Walkthrough

What is the boy doing now?

What did the boy get out of the toy box?

What might happen?

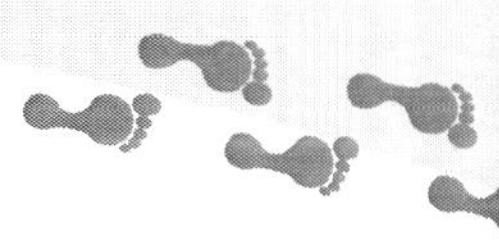

3

 **Observe and Prompt**

Language Comprehension

Check that children can:

- describe what the boy is doing and why
- identify the main change in the two pictures
- predict how the story might develop.

3

Walkthrough

What has happened?

What might Dad be saying?

What might the boy be saying?

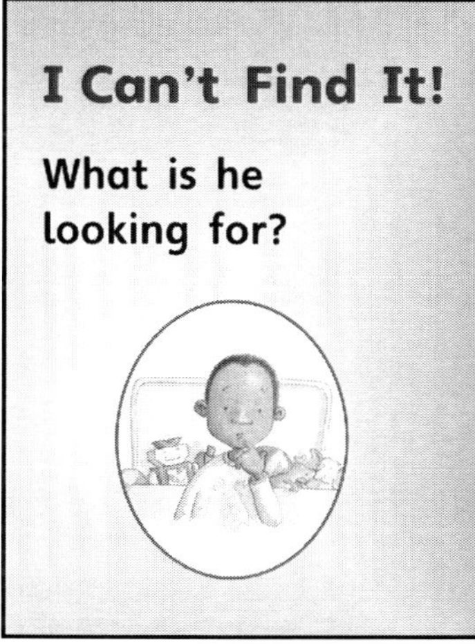

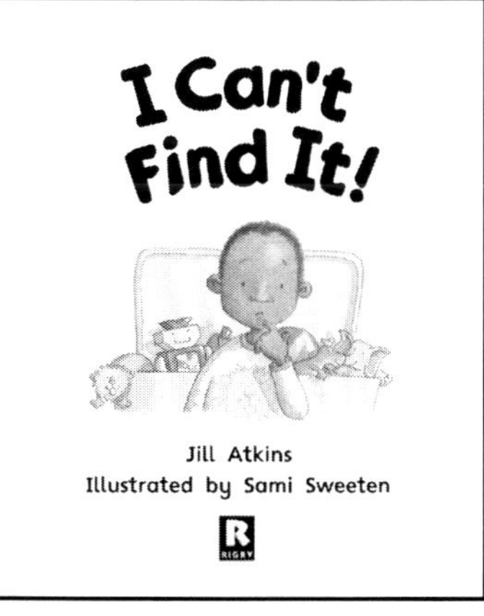

Walkthrough

This is the front cover and this is the title.

Read the title with expression, pointing to each word as you read it.

Look at the picture.

Where is the story taking place?

What might the boy have lost?

Walkthrough

This is the back cover.

This is the blurb. The blurb tells us something about the story.

Let's read it.
'What is he looking for?'

What is he thinking in the little picture?

Walkthrough

This is the title page.

Read the title again, pointing to each word.

How do you think the little boy is feeling?

What might he do next?

These are the names of the author and illustrator.

1

Walkthrough

This story is told in pictures only. The only words
are on the cover and the title page.

Where is the boy?

What is he doing?

What time of day do you think it is? Give reasons.
(*moon, night sky*)

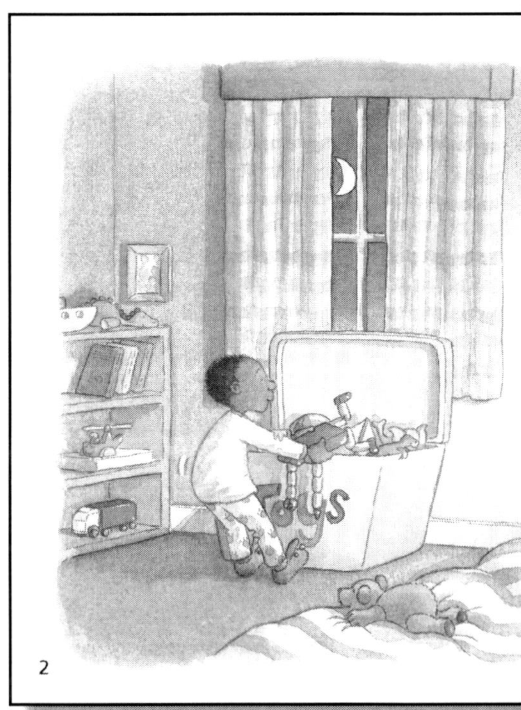

Walkthrough

What are the different characters doing?

What might Dad be saying?

What might the boy be saying?

What do the lines next to boy's head suggest?
(boy shaking his head, i.e. movement)

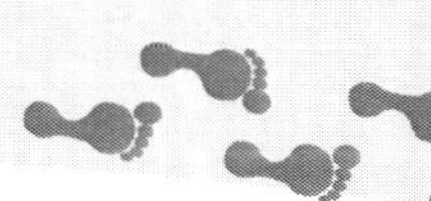

Observe and Prompt

Language Comprehension

Check that children can:

- describe what is happening in the pictures

- suggest dialogue between the boy and his dad

- notice the way the illustrator has tried to indicate movement.

Walkthrough

What is Dad doing?

What might he be saying?

What might the boy be saying?

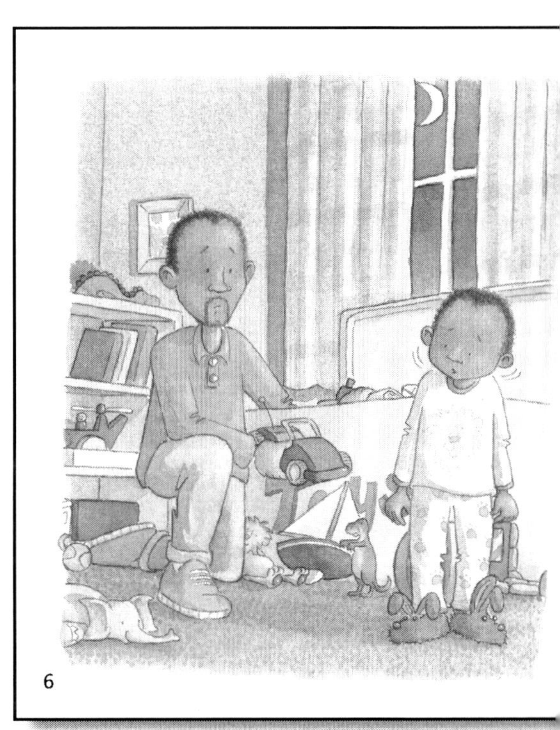

What is Dad showing the boy?

How is the boy feeling and why?

What will the two characters do next?

7

Observe and Prompt

Language Comprehension

Check that children can:

- describe what each character is doing in both pictures
- suggest what each character might be saying
- understand how the boy might be feeling
- suggest a suitable ending to the story.

Walkthrough

What is happening in the picture?

How might the boy be feeling?

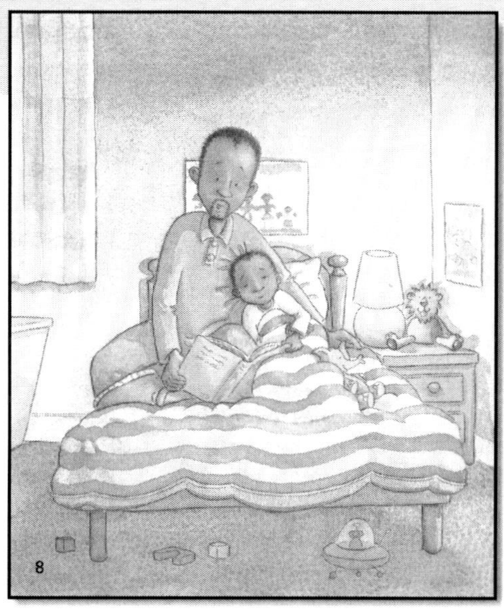

Observe and Prompt

Language Comprehension

Check that children can:

- describe what they see in the picture
- imagine what the boy is feeling now.